Barry *and his* Buddy

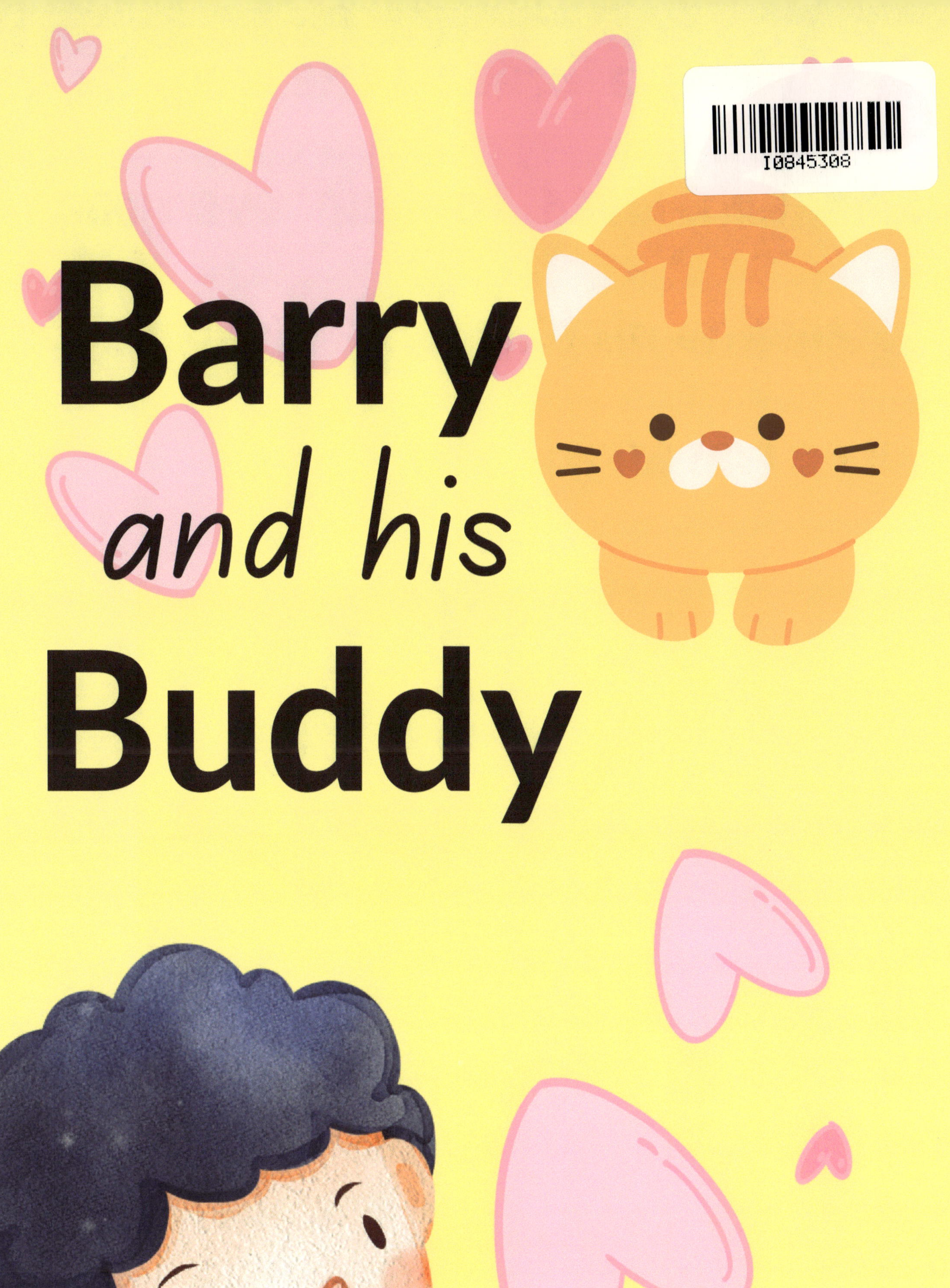

Barry was a brave little boy. He was
kind and loved to help everyone. He
listened to his teachers at school and did
all he was asked to do.

Barry loves to play soccer in the yard with his friend Peter. He also likes to ride his bike in the evening.

One Friday evening, Barry was playing with his friend, Peter. The weather was clear, and they played in Peter's yard.

Soon, the weather began to change, but they did not notice it until the rain started drizzling.

Peter's mom was busy inside, so she did not know it was beginning to rain.

Barry did not know how long the rain would fall, and since he wanted to make it home for dinner, he decided to run home before the rain became heavy.

He didn't ask Peter to lend him an umbrella either; instead, he waved his friend goodbye and ran home.

His house was close to Peter's house, so that he would get home anytime soon. However, it began to rain heavily, and Barry was soaked.

He stopped at a small shed so the rain could reduce before he continued on his way home. While he waited, he heard a cat making some sound

The cat was crying, but he did not see the cat. He paid attention to where the sound was coming from and he saw the cat.

It was wet, and its left leg was hurt. Barry felt sorry for the cat. He picked the cat up and wrapped it with his jacket.

When the rain stopped falling a while later, Barry went home.

"Barry, why did you not wait until the rain stopped or ask for an umbrella?" his mom asked.

"I did not want to wait because I was getting hungry and I did not remember to ask for an umbrella," Barry explained.

"I was worried about you. When it began to rain, I called Peter's mom, but she said you had left already".

"What do you have on your hand?" his mom noticed how he held his jacket. "I found a cat".

She was a vet. She said she would treat the cat and asked Barry to take off his wet clothes and wear a warm one.

When Barry returned a while later for dinner, his mom wrapped a bandage around the cat's leg, and it was eating.

Barry smiled at the cat and patted its head. A few days later, the cat was fine, and his mom told him it was time to return the cat.

Barry was sad because he had come to love the cat. However, he had shown his kind act to the cat, and it was time to return it to the owner.

There was no collar around the cat's neck, and when he took it to where he had found it, everyone said it was not their cat.

Barry did not want to leave the cat on the street, alone and hungry, so his mom decided that they adopt the cat.

Barry was happy. He now had a buddy. Peter also liked the cat, and they named it Honey. They played with the cat and continued being kind to humans and animals.

www.ingramcontent.com/pod-product-compliance
Lightning Source LLC
Chambersburg PA
CBHW040042240726
48664CB00003B/1030